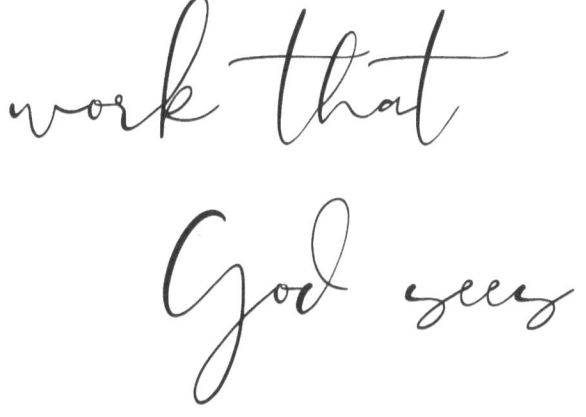

prayeful motherhood
in the midst of the overwhelm

----------------------

r e s i l i e n t

----------------------

# shannon guerra

Copyright © 2020 Shannon Guerra

All rights reserved. No part of this book may be reproduced in any form or by any electronic or mechanical means, including information storage and retrieval systems, without permission in writing from the publisher, except by reviewers, who may quote brief passages in a review.

ISBN 978-1-7345978-0-6
ISBN (ebook) 978-1-7345978-1-3

Scripture quotations are from the ESV® Bible (The Holy Bible, English Standard Version®), copyright © 2001 by Crossway, a publishing ministry of Good News Publishers. Used by permission. All rights reserved.

Portions of scripture in **bold** are the author's emphasis.

Cover design by Copperlight Wood

This title may be purchased in bulk for ministry or group study use. For more information, please email shop@copperlightwood.com.

Printed and bound in the United States of America

Published by Copperlight Wood
P.O. Box 870697
Wasilla, AK   99687

www.copperlightwood.com

For Evelyn Jean,

my grandma

who survived many fires

and emerged brighter than ever

Also by Shannon Guerra

**Upside Down:**
*Understanding and Supporting Attachment
in Adoptive and Foster Families*

**Oh My Soul:**
*Encountering God in
Honest, Unconventional
(and Sometimes Messy) Prayer*

**Oh My Soul Companion Journal**

**Oh My Soul Devotional:**
*21-Day Complete Study
3-Day Mini Studies*

**the Work That God Sees series:**
*Prayerful Motherhood
in the Midst of the Overwhelm*
**Capable
Allied
Growing
Steadfast
Resilient
Seen**

*contents*

***resilient:***
*a definition*
**7**

***to cover a multitude of sins***
**9**

***thrown a curve:***
*navigating unfamiliar territory*
**13**

***G.K. Chesterton:***
*on the meaning of brevity*
**17**

***worth fixing:***
*starting over in the middle*
**18**

***the end of the world, almost***
**22**

***us, concentrate:***
*the white egg is only prologue*
**23**

***Frederick Douglass:***
*on the necessity of struggle*
**28**

***enough:***
*what might happen if we really knew it all*
**29**

***obiter dictum:***
*observations along the way*
**32**

***no longer unclean:***
*what He does with the dirt from our past*
**33**

***what we need to hear***
*when Mother's Day is hard*
**37**

***Madeleine L'Engle:***
*on the overcoming nature of artists*
**39**

***epic:***
*who we are at the end of our story*
**40**

***easter egg dye***
*au naturel*
**47**

***questions***
*for personal journaling or group discussion*
**49**

***notes***
**52**

*resilient*

## resilient:
adjective. able to bounce back

## see also:
gritty, hardy, indefatigable,
rolling with the punches, tough,
undaunted, unshaken, unstoppable

## stronger than before

*this is who you are.*

*to cover a multitude of sins*

**We avoided ER visits** at least three times that spring day: Once, a sibling left her baby brother alone on the couch (but he didn't fall on his head), and twice, another child was caught carrying a knife the entirely wrong way (but no one was stabbed). The dryer was busted, so we were channeling our inner *Little House on the Prairie* and clothes were hanging everywhere to dry. Also, our ice maker was on the blink because it didn't like the glitter that fell into it.

We had tears during math, so I grabbed a file full of stickers – big stickers, little stickers, one sticker for every problem, I didn't care how many stickers it took as long as she found joy in it – and suddenly I realized that I need the same thing sometimes, too. Not stickers, but whatever will bring a little more joy to the day and its drama: a fresh cup of tea, a few minutes with the cat, or an hour of outside time for the kids so I can read for a while in a quiet house.

I came across this verse and, in a moment of homeschool rebellion, wrote it in our math textbook:

*Above all, keep loving one another earnestly, since love covers a multitude of sins.*

*- 1 Peter 4:8*

This verse was good news because we had a multitude of sins that day on top of the chaos I already mentioned: broken dishes, tantrums, yelling, an almost-ruined camera, blaming...I'll stop there. But if we could love each other earnestly at the end of the day, those loud memories might quiet a little under His covering, and we might have a little less chaos tomorrow.

I won't pretend it's easy, though.

We moved on from math and on to science, and my oldest son was reading about the discovery of protein structure. It was a hard process; scientists had already figured out how to find the structure of a molecule, but proteins were so much smaller and more complex that it made discovering their structure that much harder.

And I think it's sort of like how I can understand how love covers a multitude of sins, but I am still trying to learn how to consistently *stay* loving in the midst of the chaos. Not everything is solved by a handful of sticker sheets or a fresh cup of tea. So many small humans, so many complex behaviors, and I am so often out of answers, out of energy, and out of patience.

Some days are full of life-changing events that threaten to devastate us: A diagnosis. A confession. An announcement. An event that happens so fast, we don't have a chance to prepare for how it is going to shake our reality in the days to come. A multitude of sins.
Sometimes facing tomorrow is more than we think we can handle after the day we've just walked through.

"But," as my son's science book said, "some people have dozens of times more perseverance than the rest of us." [1]

And that's what I want to be: Persevering. Steadfast. But also, resilient.

If *steadfastness* is pushing through to breakthrough, *resilience* is rising again after devastation or loss. They both move forward and they often go together. We are steadfast when we have survived the waiting; we are resilient when we have survived the breaking. And there are many days when motherhood breaks us wide open.

> *Now may our Lord Jesus Christ himself, and God our Father, who loved us and gave us eternal comfort and good hope through grace, comfort your hearts and establish them in every good work and word.*
>
> *- 2 Thessalonians 2:16-17*

We moved on to a Bible lesson, and the kids and I talked about Jericho: The marching, the yelling, and the walls falling down. The obedience, the declaration, and the miracle.

"It doesn't make sense!" Chamberlain said. And she was right; it never makes sense. Marching around a city can't make walls fall down, right?

But it did, because God told them to. Obedience is powerful. Especially when it doesn't make sense.

Forgiveness doesn't always make sense. Reconciliation doesn't always make sense. Most big moves – starting a business, a mission, a family – don't always make sense. Mothering in the midst of the overwhelm, in the clutter and the mayhem and the mess, and then getting up to do it all again the next morning in spite of how the day before attempted to break us, doesn't make sense.

But here we are, you and I, doing it. Over and over again.

We can do whatever He's calling us to: Adopt, give birth, defend the helpless, write the book, heal the breach, comfort the hurting. Cover the multitude of sins, earnestly love the sinner. We can survive the breaking, and rise from ashes. We can do whatever He says.

When school was done, we got in the car. And I don't remember where we went that day, but I do remember that the trees were budding and it was in the sixties, and we drove with the windows down so everyone could hear our Alaskan kids complain about how hot it was in the Stagecoach.

But all those tiny green leaves had a sermon, and they still preach to us: In case you ever think your story is over, God has given us nature to show us that a season of bleak winter is never forever.

Go pray circles around that next step and kick up some dust, because this is how we cover the multitude of sins, and how we rise from the ashes. The Lord has given us the city.

# Thrown a Curve
## navigating unfamiliar territory

**Don't hold it against me,** but my husband is amazing at doing the laundry. Vince tackles most of it on Saturdays while I putter around the house with other projects, but even though he does the bulk of it, I'm usually the one who folds the fitted sheets.

I never realized this until one day when I pulled fresh sheets out of the closet, and they looked...well, not like I had folded them. More like they'd been used to loosely mummify someone's forearm, and then firmly stuffed into the shelf to avoid unwrapping. He later confirmed this was exactly what he'd done.

Now, if the fitted sheets in your closet look like that, I'm not judging you. I never thought fitted sheets were actually supposed to be folded once they came out of the package, but that for the remainder of their days the owners must resort to wadding them up like a fat gauze bandage. Or, like a huge replica of a salvaged roll of toilet paper after one of our cats – probably Knightley – has unrolled approximately three miles of it.

But I was nurtured by a sweet and savvy grandma who not only introduced me to Jesus but also taught me mysteries of the gospel including, but not limited to, old hymns, soup on Sundays, and the art of folding a fitted sheet. And no, height wasn't an excuse, because she was just a nudge over five feet tall. Despite the fact that I grew up thinking that *it just isn't done*, she *au contraire'd* me and showed how simple it was:

It's the pockets. Make sure they're empty – no straggling socks or unmentionables hiding in there – and just tuck them into each other. Fold over, retuck. Fold in the curved sides. Fold again, with straight sides, and done – a beautiful rectangle of linen closet goodness.

It wasn't impossible; it was amazing. Anyone can handle a flat sheet with straight sides, but the fitted sheet throws us because of the curves. Like so many tasks in life — handling the next phase of motherhood, recovering from past mistakes, or enduring grief that threatens to tear us apart — what seems to be impossible is usually just unfamiliar territory.

> *Buttercup: We'll never survive!*
>
> *Westley: Nonsense. You're only saying that because no one ever has.*
>
> *- The Princess Bride* [2]

Every endeavor we tackle has innumerable details and problems that we don't know how to solve at first. Starting a business, starting a family, starting a mission, or just starting over – we quail too early, too often, when thrown for a curve. So much is at stake in our wavering.

> *We all know the stories about how the American Revolution was a difficult and often desperate struggle. But we forget in hindsight how unlikely it was that our forefathers would succeed. Many times defeat seemed all but*

*inevitable. Yet that small band of patriot-statesmen achieved a victory against a long-established ruler of seemingly unlimited power and authority. They did so by remaining dedicated to America's cause and to each other...fighting hard at every turn...knowing that their success or failure would determine whether they, or possibly any people, would ever fight again for the great cause of self-government.*

*– Paul Ryan* [3]

We tend to mistake the unexpected, unknown, or inconvenient for the impossible. But...*au contraire:*

*And the Lord turned to him and said, "Go in this might of yours and save Israel from the hand of Midian;* **do not I send you?**" *And he said to him, "Please, Lord, how can I save Israel? Behold, my clan is the weakest in Manasseh, and I am the least in my father's house." And the Lord said to him, "But* **I will be with you,** *and you shall strike the Midianites as one man."*

*– Judges 6:14-16*

*Have I not commanded you? Be strong and courageous. Do not be frightened, and do not be dismayed, for the Lord your God is with you wherever you go.*

*– Joshua 1:9*

We face circumstances and events not bargained for on our knees. We do not know how to do this, we don't know how it's going to work out, we don't remember signing up for this. We don't know if we're strong enough.

But we do know that champions aren't made on the easy paths, where every plan goes perfectly. Roads with curves are far more beautiful than straight highways. And this is my Alaskan bias, but rugged mountain landscapes always outdo the flat, treeless prairies. People don't stop in wonder while driving through flatlands like they do when they see the mountains and valleys wrought by tension that made the earth shake and change its shape.

Your story, and my story, is more breathtaking with curves.

What we really need is someone to show us the way through the unknown. We fight the feelings and fear of *it just isn't done* with the *au contraire* of the Father who loves us and has good plans for us in the midst of the unexpected.

Pessimism insists on the shortness of human life in order to show that life is valueless.

Religion insists on the shortness of human life in order to show that life is frightfully valuable – is almost horribly valuable.

Pessimism says that life is so short that it gives nobody a chance;
religion says that life is so short that it gives everybody his final chance.

In the first case the word brevity means futility. In the second case the word brevity means opportunity.

G.K. Chesterton [4]

# worth fixing
## starting over in the middle

**On the window seat** on a rainy Saturday, I seam-ripped miles of thread from a twin-sized quilt. Almost all of the rows looked great on the top, but due to the unproductive hybrid of overenthusiasm combined with lack of experience (plus a disdain for ironing) I had neglected to check the back side of the quilt, which had accumulated several unintended nips and tucks.

There was *so much* to take out, about thirteen rows all the way across, and Iree and I took turns with the blue seam ripper. Tiny perforated lines showed where the thread had left its mark, and more than once I was tempted to just leave it and pray that no one would ever turn the quilt over to see what a mess it really was. But no...I would know. And the possibility of a toe getting caught in one of those tucks and tearing the whole quilt was enough to convince me to rip it out and start over.

So back we went. Row after row, millions of stitches. So much time. And yet, getting that far had already taken so much time. The mess and the mistakes were worth redeeming.

Starting over is hard, and starting over in the middle is harder. Whether it's a project or something bigger like a marriage, a mission, or a career, we often call situations like these "starting from scratch," but what it really is, is taking something that's broken and redeeming it.

Adoption and foster care falls into this area, too. In our house, some days the regressive behaviors take us back to those first months of bringing our kiddos home — barely verbal, not really potty trained, and full of violent fear accumulated from years of trauma in institutions that cared more about what things looked like on the surface than what was really going on underneath. In their neglect, the thoughts and patterns that built the foundation of little lives were badly patched together in all sorts of broken ways.

To some extent, we all have patterns that have to be picked out, stitch by stitch. Our lines need to be retraced in truth.

> *Do not be conformed to this world, but be transformed by the renewal of your mind, that by testing you may discern what is the will of God, what is good and acceptable and perfect.*
>
> *- Romans 12:2*

For two of our kiddos, we learned to broaden their freedoms in micro-steps so as to not create whiplash, guarding against presumptuous or destructive behavior. The dance of attachment with kids from hard places is a precarious balance between control and freedom to keep from toppling off either side. It's a cautious cha-cha ever moving forward and back, often touch-and-go as we pray boldly but move forward with care to widen the world that has had to be shrunk so small. So much has had to be taken out and replaced with healthy patterns, and the scarring is obvious when you look up close, like so many perforated lines on this seam-ripped quilt.

We learned to walk through birthdays and other milestones with strategic navigation – small nudges toward growth, watching to see what takes, because conventional steps only begat opposition and frustration. With our son, we evaluated progress by giving him a blank canvas to write on instead of quizzing him with questions, because his answers still came from a background of fear and an attitude of manipulation. For example, asking him to write his name inevitably resulted in ANDERY, ADREY, ADNEYR, or similar purposeful errors. But the real progress showed when he thought we weren't watching, and then he spelled it right every time – like on the table outside, covered in an inch of snow. A blank canvas. And when he thought we weren't looking, he wrote *ANDREY* in big letters, for all to see.

The old lines must be redrawn. Incorrect ways of connecting, messed up ways of holding ourselves together, get taken apart and remade. And this is what I thought about as I picked out my own poor stitching, while rain puddled on the dead grass and ice outside the window. Pink thread in varying lengths, brushed to the floor, no longer needed, left scars in fabric where new lines would be sewn in, holding the pieces together correctly. It does take time. But the scars aren't just the evidence of trauma; they're also proof of healing.

Redemption takes time. If you're starting over — whether with a clean slate or an ugly mess — and it's taking longer than you thought it would, that's okay. The brevity of life does not mean futility, it means opportunity.

*For here we have no lasting city, but we seek the city that is to come.*

*Now may the God of peace who brought again from the dead our Lord Jesus, the great shepherd of the sheep, by the blood of the eternal covenant,* **equip you with everything good that you may do his will,** *working in us that which is pleasing in his sight, through Jesus Christ, to whom be glory forever and ever. Amen.*

*- Hebrews 13: 14, 20-21*

I'm praying this for you, for me, for us, and all of the redemption we partner with Him in. In spite of our fumbling, He's making something beautiful.

Broken dishwasher for a family of nine.

Also known as Armageddon.

Let's just buy a new house.

*uz, concentrate*

# the white egg is only prologue

**In one of many** mom-fails, for several Easters in a row we neglected to dye eggs. I always forgot to either buy eggs, boil eggs, or buy dye. But that's okay; we usually made up for it by binging on peanut butter and chocolate eggs, instead.

(This is also a good time to confess that we have never, *ever*, dressed up for a family photo on Easter – although one year I got photos of everyone having a Nerf war in the house, so that's close, right?)

But Grandma, in her eighties, told me that she used to dye eggs all by herself every Easter until just a few years ago, just because she loved to. And if she could do that, surely I could get myself together and pull off this project.

In the spirit of not doing anything by halves (and possibly to make up for eating chocolate eggs for breakfast several Easters in a row), we went au naturel. Bowls of eggs covered the counter, all of them filled with hot water, vinegar, and some attempt at natural dye: coffee grounds, red cabbage, tomato paste, crushed blueberries, beets, turmeric, turmeric with paprika, turmeric with tea. Lots of turmeric.

White eggs go in, colored eggs come out: That was the plan.

We found that some colors dyed faster than others. Turmeric, for example, is so effective that it will not only dye eggs but also the surrounding counter and anything else it touches, and beets will dye your fingers fuchsia the moment you start to peel them.

Others need a longer time before they change anything, and sometimes the colors changed as they dried. Some eggs went in white, came out reddish, and turned to green as they oxidized. Or they came out light blue, and darkened to a beautiful turquoise.

Some of the eggs we soaked in one color and re-soaked in another; the colors were deep and the patterns were intricate, unknown galaxies. And others just didn't change at all – apparently tomato paste won't dye diddly. Those eggs came out for a rinse, unchanged after hours except for being covered with a nasty film that we scrubbed off, only to give them another bath in a different color.

But usually, the egg went in and then came out changed.

We do, too. We dye, or die, often. How many times do you feel like you've been buried over the past year?

We go through something that changes us, and walk through pain that alters our perspective. We experience something huge, for better or worse, and are washed into something that doesn't change who we are, but how we look at things. Our essence and identity are still the same – the egg is still an egg – but we know ourselves better because of it.

Sometimes the change is fast, and other times it is a slow process as we heal and make sense of things. Sometimes we go through a series of dunkings that leave us wishing we could hold someone else under the water for once, just long enough to make them uncomfortable. (No? Never mind. Maybe it's just me.)

Every time we go through a life-changing event, our colors deepen. We mature, and the baptism makes us more *us*.

We're us, concentrated. Stronger than before.

*con·cen·trate (verb):*

*to unify, converge, focus;*

*to intensify or make more pure;*

*to separate so as to improve the quality of the valuable portion.*

Even knowing this, it is still an awful, awe-full feeling to know that someone you love is about to walk through pain that they have no idea is coming. You know it will make them stronger, but you also know that strength is birthed through anguish.

The egg goes in the water: A tough announcement. News that brings heartache. The natural consequences of a choice that a loved one is just starting to step into.

> *My son, do not despise the Lord's discipline,*
>   *and do not resent his rebuke,*
> *because the Lord disciplines those he loves,*
>   *as a father the son he delights in.*
>
> *Blessed are those who find wisdom,*
>   *those who gain understanding,*
> *for she is more profitable than silver*
>   *and yields better returns than gold.*
> *She is more precious than rubies;*
>   *nothing you desire can compare with her.*
> *Long life is in her right hand;*

*in her left hand are riches and honor.*
*Her ways are pleasant ways,*
   *and all her paths are peace.*
*She is a tree of life to those who take hold of her;*
   *those who hold her fast will be blessed.*

*- Proverbs 12:11-18*

During the week leading up to His crucifixion, Jesus knew His disciples were going to misunderstand it entirely. They would also misunderstand His words, "It is finished." He knew they would dye, and die, as they walked through pain and terror for two days, soaking in hot, vinegary water. He knew what was coming for Himself and still had deep empathy for His friends, who would not realize that the third day would bring resolution and answers. Color.

They went in weak and scared, and came out fearless, bold, ready to die for truth – and the world was changed.

*Endure hardship as discipline; God is treating you as his children. For what children are not disciplined by their father? If you are not disciplined — and everyone undergoes discipline — then you are not legitimate, not true sons and daughters at all.*

*No discipline seems pleasant at the time, but painful. Later on, however, it produces a harvest of righteousness and peace for those who have been trained by it.*

*- Hebrews 12:7-8, 11*

The eggs went in, white. Beautiful and uniform, but all pretty much the same. Then they all got buried, bathed, baptized, in a new color – and no one would ever describe them as "common" again.

Jesus knew the joy that was coming for them. He knew they would be stronger.

The white egg is only prologue. Life happens and we soak in the dye as we die to self, sometimes again and again and again. You are the valuable portion being set apart, made more pure. And suddenly, there is revelation. Joy and life. Color and complexity.

And we are us, concentrated: Stronger than ever.

If there is no struggle, there is no progress.
Those who profess to favor freedom
and yet deprecate agitation are men who want
crops without plowing up the ground;
they want rain without thunder and lightning.
They want the ocean without the awful
roar of its many waters.
This struggle may be a moral one,
or it may be a physical one,
and it may be both moral and physical,
but it must be a struggle.
Power concedes nothing without a demand.
It never did and it never will.

Frederick Douglass [5]

# enough
## what might happen if we really knew it all

**It was almost perfect.** Three kids were taking naps upstairs while everyone else finished school for the week: One kid was on the couch reading *Kidnapped*, one kid was reading *Paddle to the Sea* to her sister, and another kid was having an introvert moment, taking refuge from everyone else in the nook under the stairs.

But, as I said, it was only *almost* perfect. Just as a bubble pops the second you catch it, something crashed in the kitchen right then. Someone had put the dish of cat food on the counter, and Knightley knocked it to the floor where Bingley, her co-conspirator, was waiting. Those little sinners.

And in full disclosure, the entire day was far from perfect. One kiddo spent it cleaning bodily fluids from accidents-on-purpose, and I was emotionally wiped out from the attachment issues, the laundry, the brave face, and the tough love. Or, you could call it the poop, the pee, and the pushaway.

Not all days were like this. Some were less extreme (some were more) but often on hard days I wondered if it was enough. If I was enough. Had we done enough, were we doing enough, when it seemed like there was nothing to show for it?

*We bear fruit in two ways: inwardly in our character and outwardly in our ministry and service to others.*

*- International House of Prayer* [6]

In our laundry room windowsill stood a dark green wine bottle, filled with water and a small plant cutting. The leaves had all either fallen off or been eaten by kittens, and all that was left above the water was a stubby stem – not much to show for all the years it had sat in the water. But it was alive. And underneath the water, the roots were several feet long.

Are we enough? If you and I were sitting at the table with coffee in hand – or with our hands covered in potting soil and dirty dishes – and you asked me this, I'd tell you without any doubt in my mind that, ***Yes**, you are enough*. And I would be right. You are enough for everything He's called you to: In marriage, motherhood, work, and ministry, I'm confident you are transforming the lives of those around you as you follow Him. The kingdom is bigger and bolder because you are in it.

It's different when we ask ourselves, though.

On hard days, it's a terrible question. The roots are deep but there's not always much above ground to show for it. Like a mama who is nine months pregnant and doing everything she can to speed up labor, there are some things you can do to help things along when we are fighting for breakthrough, but in the end, that baby is only going to come when he or she is ready. And the time of birth is not up to us.

On those days, in the midst of the lying and the Lysol, I wondered if it was enough to have brought two kids out of an orphanage only for them to continue to struggle with special needs and behavioral issues. Is it enough to have protected them from trafficking and death, if they won't be healed from wounds that were embedded in utero and beyond?

And I know it is. I knew it then and I know it now. But on hard days, we want more than just enough.

*There is so much more, Love*, He told me. *But if you knew it all, you would take credit for too much. So remember what you do know, and be content with that. It is enough.*

*You are enough. I am enough for you, for all of you, for all that I'm doing in each of you.*

We grow deep and wide under the surface in our behind-the-scenes, and we grow deep and wide above the ground in what people see. Below are roots, above are shoots, and a new season will come that plants us in new ground. That will be the time to show what our roots have prepared us for.

# obiter dictum:
## observations along the way

••••••••••••••••••••••

Mercy is not boxing the ears of the child who woke the baby up from his nap while you were only halfway done with the dishes.
Justice is making him scrub all the pots and pans for doing so.

••••••••••••••••••••••

Toddler hacks babyproofing to the lazy susan: slight chaos. Toddler learns how to open containers of baking powder and animal crackers: total and utter bedlam.

••••••••••••••••••••••

Fun fact: a 9-month-old's wingspan can take up 85% of the width in a queen sized bed. #yaycoffee

••••••••••••••••••••••

Springtime hack: Tell the kids that the more they play outside, the sooner the snow will melt so the grass can grow. When that stops working, tell them to hurry up and enjoy the snow before it's gone.
This ought to buy you at least a few weeks.

••••••••••••••••••••••

Dear recipe writers: When adding the words "dark chocolate" to your ingredient list, it is never necessary to add the word "optional."
It's not like we're talking about walnuts.

# no longer unclean
## what He does with the dirt from our past

**All my life** I've lived around seagulls, and I've never noticed this until recently: They're white against the mountains, but black against the overcast sky. They make their way inland as far as we are but don't touch down near our house, preferring the litter of parking lots to the noise and activity of our kids.

We were digging compost in the garden that day. The raised beds were mostly planted, except for the one on the side of the yard where it's shadier, full of what we used to think was dill until last summer when, in July, we finally recognized our error. Once it bloomed, we realized it was in fact *not* dill, but *daisies* that Iree planted the year before. And we had been harvesting it, adding it to our baked potatoes and pasta salad.

We're still alive, so apparently daisies are not poisonous. Also, they go pretty well with salmon. Now you know.

Iree dug them up and moved them a few weeks ago to make room in the raised bed for real vegetables. But before she planted new seeds, we filled the bed with compost and covered it all up with a thin layer of plain dirt to hide the mess of black muck, rotting veggie peels, and egg shells we put in there to help make up for the shade. We hoped the compost would give the new garden a fair shot at growing.

It's what He does with us, right? Sometimes it stinks, but God uses our rotten past all the time as fertilizer to give us a fair shot at growth, too.

All our lives we've lived with some black mark. You name it – a murky past, an abusive relationship, a mental illness, an irrational fear, whatever – and it tries to touch down with its litter and filth when we attempt to step out boldly from our comfort zone.

*You're not good enough for this.*

*You've never been able to do this before.*

*If your old crowd knew what you're thinking, they'd laugh at you.*

*You only want this for the wrong reasons.*

*No one's going to cover for you when you fail.*

All lies. Half-truths, maybe, but those are just lies with pretty clothes on – they're still lies. Because when He washes us and we start over, we're no longer unclean.

We're uncommon.

*But the voice answered a second time from heaven, "What God has made clean, do not call common."*

*- Acts 11:9*

We've never noticed that those black marks flying over us change color against a stronger background. When looked at with the enemy's overcast perspective, they're bleak smudges, but when we see them from God's perspective of strength, healing, and triumph over the mountains we've climbed, they are white.

*Hey, Love,* He says, *you have more gifts than you're aware of.* [7]

*It's time for you to try to use them and flex those muscles long unused. [8]*

*You have no idea how many people are cheering you on. [9]*

*When you spend time with Me, your dreams reflect it. [10]*

*I have your back. [11]*

They are light accents, not black marks against our clouded history. They're the experiences of broken humility that taught us to show grace to others. They're the muck that strong character came out of. They're the chisels that carved us – painful as it was, and as it still is sometimes – and now we look more like Him.

It doesn't always work, of course. A heart that wants to move on and produce fruit is better ground for growth than a heart that festers over old wounds and never gets past the point of decay. But He always offers the potential to grow more because of it. It's our choice.

In God's frugal economy of never wasting a thing, He makes up for the shade and redeems the pain with augmented healing and maturity, often bearing mature fruit earlier or larger than if we'd had a "hothouse variety" Christian experience, not knowing the root-deepening experiences of life outside the greenhouse.

Please don't think I'm knocking greenhouses. In many ways we try to provide a more (ahem) temperate environment for our own kids than what we had. But we know the value of prayerful hardening off, too – it's necessary for strengthening roots and teaching our saplings to turn toward the sun instead of depending on artificial grow lights.

Iree ended up planting that garden bed full of unidentified mystery seeds from the bottom of our gardening bucket – the remnants of various packets dropped upside down by the chubby hands of inattentive gardeners. A medley of potential, a veggie surprise. We have no idea how they will handle the shade, but we know they're planted in the richest dirt we can give them. Just like our kids.

Even at the end of the day, in the wee hours of the morning as I'm showering off the last 16 hours, I need His words all over again. Our days fall short of perfect and we have to fend off the circling, hovering, and pecking attacks. We want to say the right thing but we run out of patience. We want our kids to be best friends, but they fight. We want them to adore us as parents, when that adoration really belongs to God. They need to know that we know we're still not perfect, even though we want to be.

Deep breath. It's okay, Mama. *What you're doing is hard, but you're doing a good job.*

God is constantly taking the mud that the enemy throws at us to use for our benefit: To turn us into people who lead our kids well, who love each other well, and who pursue Him well. For our joy, He turns darkness into light.

## what we need to hear
## when Mother's Day is hard

**For those who dread** Mother's Day – whether because of death, abuse, estrangement, infertility, fear, miscarriage, abortion, ingratitude, mistakes or any other thing:

I wish I could tell you that if you're not ready for it, you don't have to go to church that day. That if it brings more pain and damage, you don't have to make that phone call. That if it's not genuine, you don't have to put on the happy face and pretend like everything is okay when you know you are lying when you act like it is. That you don't have to fake it when the day is more painful than celebratory.

But really, I can't tell you that. We are adults, we have responsibilities, we have children who need us and churches we serve in. There are some things we absolutely must do. Other things, we absolutely must not do. He gives wisdom to each of us.

What I can tell you is that it's okay to grieve. It's okay to recognize that this is the hardest day of the year for some of us, and some years, the grief piles on from several directions. It's okay to admit that life doesn't always match a happy Hallmark card.

But what I most want to tell you is that your Father loves you, and He longs to heal you. He makes those strong in His strength who face grief through His eyes.

Even after pruning. Even after a hard winter. He is in the business of making all things new.

It is interesting to note how many artists have had physical problems to overcome, deformities, lameness, terrible loneliness. Could Beethoven have written that glorious paean of praise in the Ninth Symphony if he had not had to endure the dark closing in of deafness? As I look through his work chronologically, there's no denying that it deepens and strengthens along with the deafness.

Could Milton have seen all that he sees in Paradise Lost if he had not been blind? It is chastening to realize that those who have no physical flaw, who move through life in step with their peers, who are bright and beautiful, seldom become artists. The unending paradox is that we do learn through pain.

Madeleine L'Engle [12]

*epic*

# who we are at the end of our story

**You've probably heard** of this guy, Maewyn Succat.

No? Trust me, you know him. You've probably even celebrated him. Let me give you a hint: Shamrocks, green clothing, beer. Maybe green beer. He has a holiday named after him, often involving green beer.

See, I told you — we know him as St. Patrick. But most of us don't know his story; we don't know what happened to make a kid named Maewyn Succat become a saint named Patrick. It's worth knowing, though:

> *St. Patrick was a Roman Briton of good family dwelling probably in the Severn valley. His father was a Christian deacon, a Roman citizen, and a member of the municipal council. One day in the early fifth century there descended on the district a band of Irish raiders, burning and slaying.* [13]

Well, that sounds terrible. The enemy was up to no good. It's an awful part of our history.

*The young Patrick was carried off and sold into slavery —*

It gets worse and worse. But the sentence isn't finished yet, and the last two words reveal much about the rest of the story.

*The young Patrick was carried off and sold into slavery **in Ireland**.* [14]

And we know that God was up to something, too. Regardless of what the enemy was trying to destroy, God was doing what He always does – creating redemption in an all-things-for-good, beauty-for-ashes, Romans 8:28,[15] epic kind of way. In between the boy and the saint, God hovered: protecting, watching, guiding, taking every attack from the enemy and turning it on its head. He was making history through this young man.

*For six years...he tended swine, and loneliness led him to seek comfort in religion. He was led by miraculous promptings to attempt escape.*

*Although many miles separated him from the sea he made his way to a port, found a ship, and persuaded the captain to take him on board.*

*After many wanderings we find him in one of the small islands off Marseilles, then a centre of the new monastic movement spreading westward from the Eastern Mediterranean...*

**He conceived an earnest desire to return good for evil and spread the tidings he had learned among his former captors in Ireland.** [16]

He didn't just sail back to Ireland immediately, though. He obeyed, waited, and let God mold him into the saint that would save a nation.

*After fourteen years of careful training by the Bishop and self-preparation for what must have seemed a forlorn adventure Patrick sailed back in 432 to the wild regions which he had quitted.* ***His success was speedy and undying.*** *17*

And I want to share this with those of you who are fighting discouragement over terrible attack, an awful history, and an uncertain future. The enemy can try to create a plot twist, but God writes the best stories for those who let Him.

*Now I rejoice in my sufferings for your sake, and in my flesh I am filling up what is lacking in Christ's afflictions for the sake of his body, that is, the church, of which **I became a minister according to the stewardship from God that was given to me for you, to make the word of God fully known, the mystery hidden for ages and generations but now revealed to his saints.** To them God chose to make known how great among the Gentiles are the riches of the glory of this mystery, which is Christ in you, the hope of glory. Him we proclaim, warning everyone and teaching everyone with all wisdom, that we may present everyone mature in Christ.*

*– Colossians 1:24-28*

There is nothing He can't do with a person who trusts Him utterly — unflinching in obedience, uncowed by the enemy, unchained to the comfort zone, and unhindered by society's expectations.

*The world does not need super-men, but supernatural men. Men who will persistently turn the self out of their lives and let Divine Power work through them.* [18]

Let's do another one. There was this girl: She was young, but she'd been on adventures.

She was the daughter of a king and had risked her life to protect the enemy of her people. She was abducted for ransom, but deemed not worth saving by her royal father. Eventually she married into the enemy's camp and sailed with her husband to another country, where she lived in a completely foreign culture and died three years later.

Her name was Rebecca Rolfe, but that's not the name she's known for. She's known for the name she had earlier, when she did that amazing thing she is celebrated for – saving the life of John Smith. Her name then, of course, was Pocahontas.

*For consider your calling, brothers: not many of you were wise according to worldly standards, not many were powerful, not many were of noble birth. But God chose what is foolish in the world to shame the wise; God chose what is weak in the world to shame the strong.*

*– 1 Corinthians 1:26-27*

There was this other girl: the daughter of a political activist who was assassinated when she was a child in the early 1900's.

She was born in a small eastern European country that had its own identity crisis to such an extent that she technically had several nationalities by the time she reached adulthood. She gave all those up though, and moved away, eventually to become a legal citizen of the country she served, lived, and died in.

Her name at birth was Agnes Bojaxhiu, but the name everyone revered at her death was Mother Teresa.

> *God chose what is low and despised in the world, even things that are not, to bring to nothing things that are, so that no human being might boast in the presence of God. And because of him you are in Christ Jesus, who became to us wisdom from God, righteousness and sanctifica- tion and redemption, so that, as it is written, "Let the one who boasts, boast in the Lord."*
>
> *– 1 Corinthians 1:28-31*

There was a man named Paul, formerly Saul, trans-formed from persecutor to apostle. His story wreaks fear in the enemy who would like to see people chained to their past.

> *I thank Him who has given me strength, Christ Jesus our Lord, because He judged me faithful, appointing me to His service, **though former-ly I was a blasphemer, persecutor, and insolent opponent.** But I received mercy because I had acted ignorantly in unbelief, and the grace of our Lord overflowed for me with the faith and love that are in Christ Jesus.*
>
> *The saying is trustworthy and deserving of full acceptance, that **Christ Jesus came into the world to save sinners, of whom I am the foremost.***

***But I received mercy for this reason,*** *that in me, as the foremost,* ***Jesus Christ might display His perfect patience as an example*** *to those who were to believe in Him for eternal life.*

*To the King of the ages, immortal, invisible, the only God, be honor and glory forever and ever. Amen.*

*– 1 Timothy 1:12-17*

Our history does not dictate our future. He's not done with us, and He's not done with those we've been praying for, either — the hurting child, the struggling teen, the difficult coworker, the angry relative, the grieving friend, the immoral business owner, the dishonest politician.

(I've heard He even saves people who voted for Clinton in the 90's – though Vince is quick to remind me that love keeps no record of wrongs.)

Who we will be at the end of our story is still being shaped by our willingness to obey and follow Him. Our future is still being written. What will we be known for?

*They will see His face, and His name will be on their foreheads. And night will be no more. They will need no light of lamp or sun, for the Lord God will be their light, and they will reign forever and ever.*

*– Revelation 22:4-5*

None of these people could have known what the ending of their stories would be when God spoke to them in the beginning of their journeys.

And at the end of our story, we will look back and notice the same thing.

For anyone feeling tied to their past, and for all of us in the middle of the story, between a rock and a hard place, not sure how this thing ends: God creates all things new, leaves no stone unturned, leaves no person untouched. At the end of your story, He will call you by your name, and say, *Hey, Love, this is who you are.*

God isn't done with you yet. He is hovering over you: protecting, watching, guiding, and taking every attack from the enemy and turning it on its head. Prepare for something epic. It will be the story of your life.

# easter egg dye
## au naturel

**I won't lie,** this isn't easier than plopping little commercial tablets into cups of water for predictably perfect color results. But it *is* fun, even for mamas like me who hate messy kitchen projects. (Oh shoot. Did I just type that out loud?)

**What you need (besides patience):**
*A bunch of hard boiled eggs*
*Several large containers to soak the ingredients and eggs in.* I like glass bowls so you can see the colors and how many eggs are hidden in there.
*White vinegar*
*Boiling water*
*Large spoons,* preferably slotted
*A cardboard egg crate*, or other safe, absorbent place to deposit eggs to dry

*Essential ingredients for dyeing:* **Powdered turmeric** for yellow, **red cabbage** (thinly sliced) for blue, and **beets** (also thinly sliced) for red.

These three items will give you the primary colors, and you can combine them however you want for a million other colors. But other ingredients are fun to try, too, like spinach, blueberries, black tea, carrots, or overdue fee notices from the library. You know, just whatever you happen to have an abundance of.

**Directions:**

1. Distribute your dyeing ingredients among the large containers. This is a good time for the kids to argue about who gets to make green, how much to allot for red, and whether or not red cabbage really will create blue. (Or, just do this on your own while they play outside. You do not, I repeat, NOT, want them to get beet dye all over your house.)

2. Fill each container halfway with boiling water.

3. Add 2 tablespoons of white vinegar to each container.

4. Let the dyeing commence: Go ahead and add the eggs to the water with the dye ingredients, which help cushion the shells from cracking when overzealous dye-ers keep pulling them out and dropping them in again after repeated checking.

This is another good time for the kids to argue about who is hogging the yellow, who has already dyed more eggs than anyone else, and – *OH MY GOSH, the red cabbage really DOES turn eggs blue!!* Try not to gloat too much over it.

## for personal journaling or group discussion

### to cover a multitude of sins:

What are three small things I can do for myself to bring a little more joy to my day and its drama?

What are three small things I can do for my kids to bring more joy and peace to their day?

What do I need to do in this season that doesn't make sense: Forgiveness, restoration, a big move? How can I pray circles around that thing? What is my first step of obedience?

### thrown a curve:

What curves in my life have made my story more beautiful? What curves have been ugly, but were used by God to make me stronger, and make my story more breathtaking?

What used to seem unfamiliar and impossible to me, but is now within my comfort zone?

What is currently unfamiliar (and possibly intimidating) to me that God is calling me toward? What would feeling comfortable/familiar/at peace with that look like?

### us, concentrate:

What have I experienced recently that changed the way I look at things?

How do I know myself better because of it? How do I know God better because of it?

What am I going through right now that makes me uncommon, and is teaching me to be stronger than ever?

### enough:

What breakthrough(s) am I contending for in this season?

What victories in my life might I have taken credit for if they came too easy?

How is God growing me underground, behind the scenes, while I wait and pray?

### no longer unclean:

What black marks or rotten things in my past has God redeemed into places of growth, strength, and triumph? What mud from my past has God turned to my benefit?

Is there any area where my heart does not want to move on, and has been festering over old wounds, instead? How can I start praying into that?

What lies/half-truths has the enemy been giving me? What is God's truth in those areas?

## epic:

How can I prepare now for the bigger-than-my-imagination exploits that God might be strengthening me for?

What do I want people to say about me at the end of my story?

What do I want to say about others who I've been praying for, at the end of their story?

1. Michael J. Behe, *Darwin's Black Box* (New York: Free Press, 1996), 12.

2. *The Princess Bride*. Directed by Rob Reiner (Century City, CA: Twentieth Century Fox, 1987, DVD).

3. Paul Ryan, quoted from *Imprimis*, July/August 2014 (reprinted by permission from Imprimis, a publication of Hillsdale College).

4. G.K. Chesterton, introduction to *Nicholas Nickleby* by Charles Dickens (New York: Everyman's Library, 1993) 835.

5. Frederick Douglass, "West India Emancipation," speech. Canandaigua, NY, August 3, 1857.

6. International House of Prayer. 2016. "We bear fruit in two ways: inwardly in our character and outwardly in our ministry and service to others." Facebook, February 26, 2016.

7. *Blessed be the God and Father of our Lord Jesus Christ, who has blessed us in Christ with every spiritual blessing in the heavenly places.* (Ephesians 1:3)

8. *I can do all things through him who strengthens me.* (Philippians 4:13)

9. *Therefore, since we are surrounded by so great a cloud of witnesses, let us also lay aside every weight, and sin which clings so closely, and let us run with endurance the race that is set before us.* (Hebrews 12:1)

10. *Delight yourself in the Lord, and he will give you the desires of your heart.* (Psalm 37:4)

11. *Jesus looked at them and said, "With man it is impossible, but not with God. For all things are possible with God."* (Mark 10:27)

12. Madeleine L'Engle, *Walking On Water* (Colorado Springs, CO: WaterBrook Press, 2001), 67-68.

13. Winston Churchill, *The Birth of Britain* (New York: Barnes & Noble, Inc., by arrangement with Dodd, Mead, & Company, Inc., 2005), 61.

14. Ibid.

15. *And we know that for those who love God all things work together for good, for those who are called according to his purpose.* (Romans 8:28)

16. Winston Churchill, *The Birth of Britain* (New York: Barnes & Noble, Inc., by arrangement with Dodd, Mead, & Company, Inc., 2005), 61-62.

17. Ibid, 62.

18. *God Calling*, ed. A.J. Russell (Ulrichsville, Ohio: Barbour Publishing, 1998), entry titled "February 15."

# Also by Shannon Guerra

"What makes this book stand out from other contemporary Christian writings on prayer is the author's crisp prose and sharp sense of humor... An insightful, honest, and genuinely funny author delivers a standout devotional."

- *Kirkus Reviews*

*It's significant that paper is made from the same material He was nailed to. He still uses it to heal us, show us more of Him, and conquer what's harassing us.*

Available wherever books are sold, and at **copperlightwood.com**

Adoptive and foster families often feel alone, but it doesn't have to be that way. Shannon Guerra learned this first-hand after she and her husband adopted two children in 2012, and she started writing shockingly transparent blog posts about what her family was going through at home, at the doctor's office, and in her heart as a mama.

And adoptive and foster families started writing back.

Their overwhelming, unanimous theme was, "This is what I've wanted to tell people for so long. **I wish everyone who knows our family could read this.**"

*Upside Down* is the result. Because adoptive & foster families should never feel alone, & communities can be equipped to make sure they never feel that way again.

*one more thing...*

Do you want more encouragement in the season you're in? Do you want to grow deep and wide, regardless of your space and circumstances?

You are warmly invited to copperlightwood.com where we're transparent about finding peace in the hard moments, beauty in the mess, and white space in the chaos. It's a little unpolished here, so watch out for the Legos on the floor.

His peace is for you,

Shannon Guerra

**subscribe:**
eepurl.com/MugpP

**connect:**
instagram.com/copperlightwood
facebook.com/copperlightwood
goodreads.com/shannonguerra

www.ingramcontent.com/pod-product-compliance
Lightning Source LLC
Chambersburg PA
CBHW021133080526
44587CB00012B/1262